The Remarkable, Adaptable Turtle

Written by Susan McCloskey

Celebration Press

Parsippany, New Jersey

Mississippi Map Turtle

Loggerhead Sea Turtle

Texas Tortoise

Leatherback Turtle

Turtles have been on the earth since the time of the dinosaurs—nearly 200 million years. Crocodiles, lizards, and snakes are the only other reptiles that have been around this long.

How have turtles survived for so long?

Green Sea Turtle

Galapagos Tortoise

Star Tortoise

Eastern Box Turtle

Most turtles have a hard shell. The shell protects the turtle from the sharp teeth and claws of other animals, such as skunks and raccoons.

Many turtles can pull their heads, legs, and tails into their shells. That makes it hard for other animals to harm them. Some turtles even have parts of their shells that work like hinges on a door. These parts swing closed after the turtle has pulled its body parts inside. Then the turtle is almost as safe as a rock!

Some turtles also have other ways of protecting themselves. The musk turtle sprays a bad smelling scent when enemies, like snakes, birds, or people, come near.

The snapping turtle has a large head and strong, sharp jaws. It raises itself up and snaps its jaws when it is threatened. It has a fierce bite.

ecause turtles have adapted to their changing environment so well, they can live almost anywhere. They need only food, water, soft dirt or mud to burrow under, and a few months of warm weather.

Turtles need some warm weather because they are reptiles. Like other reptiles, such as snakes and lizards, turtles are cold-blooded. Their body temperature doesn't stay warm, as ours does. Their body temperature is about the same as that of the air or water around them.

If the air temperature is warm, the turtle is warm. If the air is cold, the turtle is cold. When a turtle is very cold, its blood slows down and it cannot move to find food. That's why most turtles cannot live where it is cold all year long.

So where do turtles go when winter comes? Land turtles, also called tortoises, bury themselves in dirt, mud, or rotting plants, and sleep there for the winter. This is called hibernation.

Many sea turtles, such as the loggerhead, live in warm waters, so they do not need to hibernate. The leatherback sea turtle, which lives in colder waters, is able to stay warm because of its huge size. It has an outer layer of tough skin over its shell and more fat than other turtles. These help to keep it warm.

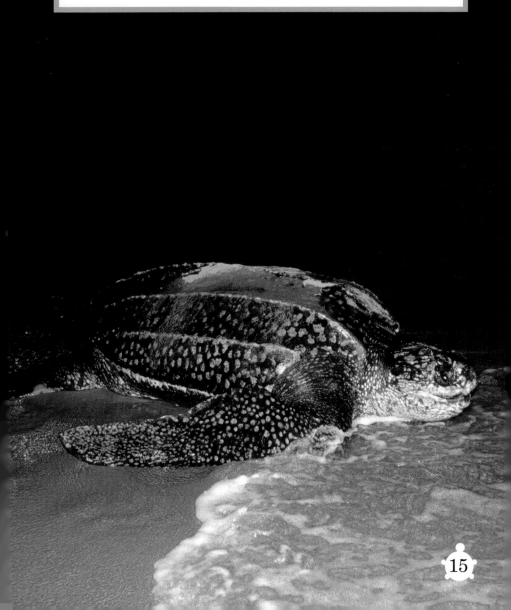

Although many sea turtles are big, the biggest turtle ever found was a leatherback. It weighed almost 2,000 pounds. Leatherbacks can be nearly eight feet long.

Sea turtles are wonderful swimmers. They can swim much faster and farther than people can! They use their strong front flippers like paddles. They use their back flippers to steer and stop. Green sea turtles have been known to swim distances of up to 1,400 miles to lay their eggs!

All turtles—whether they live on land or in water—lay their eggs on land. The female turtle digs a hole with her back legs. After she lays her eggs in the hole, she covers them up. When the eggs hatch, the babies crawl out—all on their own.

Now they must feed and protect themselves. As baby sea turtles make their way toward the water, many are eaten by birds or other small animals. Fish are also waiting to eat them when they reach the water.

Turtles, like other reptiles, don't need to eat every day. Instead, they eat lots of food when it is available. This food is stored in their fat. Then they can go for days or weeks without eating.

Turtles eat a variety of things. Some eat mostly plants. Others eat only meat. But most will eat lots of things, either plants or meat.

The green sea turtle is a plant eater. It eats mainly sea grass. The grass turns the turtle's fat green. This is why it is called the green sea turtle, although many green sea turtles have brown shells!

The alligator snapping turtle is a meat eater. It lies on the bottom of a river with its mouth wide open. The end of its tongue looks like a worm. The turtle goes fishing by wiggling the "worm." A fish sees it and swims right into the turtle's jaws. What an easy meal for the turtle!

Whatever they eat, turtles cannot chew it. That's because they have no teeth. They use their strong, hard beaks to chop and tear at their food.

It's easy to understand why turtles have been on the earth for such a long time. Their shells protect them. They can live almost anywhere. They can eat many different things.

But will turtles be around in another 200 million years? That may depend on us.

Today there are fewer turtles than there used to be. Many species are endangered. One reason is that people are using the land and water where turtles once lived. We need to work to protect the places where turtles still live. If we do, turtles may still be around for a long time.